THIS IS FUN!

Expanding the Language Experience Through:

EFL/ESL
CLASS STARTERS

with Activities and Blackline Masters

CRISTINA LARIS

Barbara Hojel
EFL/ESL Consultant

SCOTT, FORESMAN AND COMPANY
Editorial Office   Glenvi

Regional Offices   Sun
Glenview, Illinois • Oal

ISBN: 0-673-19199-0

3 4 5 6 EBI 99 98

Contents

This Is Fun!

This Is Fun! is a series of books designed to help teachers of English as a foreign or second language plan lessons that will engage and maintain students' attention, encourage their participation, and provide a wide variety of language experiences. The materials and activities in the series make it possible for the EFL/ESL teacher to help children acquire their new language in much the same manner they learned their mother tongue—by using the language in enjoyable and meaningful ways.

The materials in each book of the series are arranged according to topic (school, home, family, birthdays, weather, calendar, etc.). By choosing activities from one or more of the books, a teacher can plan units that develop basic language skills according to his or her own needs and preferences as well as the needs and preferences of the class.

The ideas in these books can be used to supplement and enrich any English as foreign or second language program. They are equally effective as warm-ups at the beginning of class, as quick changes of pace to maintain students' attention, or as enjoyable follow-up activities after drill or practice. The wide variety of materials and activities will not only help develop students' knowledge and understanding of English, they will make any class or program come alive.

EFL/ESL Class Starters

The first few minutes of any class are the most important because they set the tone for the rest of the day. Therefore, if we want our students to participate and to speak in English, we should start our classes with activities which encourage them to do just that.

This book contains many activities that you can use to begin your class. Some will be more appropriate than others, depending on the age and level of language skills of your students. Choose those activities that you think you and your students will enjoy the most, but don't feel that you must do only those activities for an entire year, or even for a whole month or week! The activities will be successful only as long as you and your students are interested in them. Whenever interest in an activity wanes, you will want to switch to another of the many ideas in this book.

A wide variety of activities and materials will help keep your students' attention. For example, you will probably not want to do a Daily News activity and a TV Newscast activity on the same day. Although the materials and activities in these sections are very different, the main idea is similar, and students might lose interest. It would be wiser to choose an activity from Daily News and one from How Do You Feel? or from Fun With Numbers to do on any one day.

The most important things to consider when you choose the activities for your class are the age and interests of your students. When children are interested, they will find it fun to participate, and they will speak in English. And that's what this book is all about!

How To Use This Book

This book is divided into fifteen sections—Attendance, Calendar, Color of the Week, Shapes, Show and Tell, Surprise Box, Happy Birthday!, Weather, On the Way to School, Observing Our World, Fun With Numbers, How Do You Feel?, Daily News, TV Newscast, and This Is Fun Club. These are topics which interest children of all ages, so they are great for the start of class. Many activities are suggested within each topic, so you can choose the ones you believe will be both interesting and fun for your students and for yourself.

You will probably find it useful to take a few minutes right now to look through the book to get an over-all idea of the activities it contains. Mark those that you think will work best for you in your particular situation.

After you have made your preliminary selections, check to see what materials are needed for those activities. Think about how you will arrange the materials and proceed with the activities before you make your final choice.

Throughout the book, there are sections marked ▶. These are teaching tips that you will find useful both as you present the material in this book and during the rest of your teaching day.

Within many of the activities, you will find indented questions and sentences. These highlight conversation activities and give examples of what you and your students might say. They will remind you to model any responses necessary and, most of all, to encourage the children to talk!

▶ The most important thing to remember to have a successful class is to consider your students' ages and interests. If the activities you choose are too difficult or are not appropriate, the children won't be excited about participating. And if they don't want to participate, you've lost before you've even started!

Materials

It's very important that you use materials that children like and find interesting. Many of the materials you will need to do the activities in this book are included as blackline masters. Duplicate these pages and use them. Add your own ideas.

▶ Let your students make materials for your class. When the children participate in making materials, drawing charts, putting up bulletin boards, etc., they feel important and enjoy contributing to the class. (This helps you out, too!)

Whenever you need specific materials for an activity (pens, boxes, rags, etc.), be sure they're available and ready to be used. The fastest way to lose your students' interest and attention is to make them wait while you find flash cards, tape, or pins!

Put envelopes or boxes near your bulletin board so you can keep materials where you need them. Be sure that any charts you make will fit on the bulletin board *before* you make them. Keep pictures or flash cards in an alphabetical file so you can find the right one easily.

If you don't have a convenient bulletin board, think of alternate ways to do an activity. Be creative. Use an easel. Cover a piece of thick cardboard with cloth, paint, or adhesive plastic. Display things on large boxes or along the chalkrail. Look around your classroom. What other things and places can you use?

▶ Take the extra time to have all the materials ready before you start your class. You will notice the difference!

Classroom Management

Classroom Rules
All students find it easier to work in class when they know what's expected of them. Take time at the beginning of the year to organize your class. Begin by establishing Classroom Rules.

Allow your students to contribute to the rule-making as much as possible. We are all more likely to follow rules we have made ourselves rather than rules imposed on us by others.

▶ Make the Classroom Rules short and easy to understand. And don't make too many! Three or four rules are easier to remember and obey than nine or ten!

State the rules in a positive rather than a negative way. Don't say *No running in this class.* For positive reinforcement, say *We walk in our classroom. We speak in soft voices* is better than *No shouting allowed.* (Remember that what you think is a soft voice may not be the same as what your students think is a soft voice. Demonstrate the proper tone so students understand right away.)

As you and your students decide on each rule, write it on a chart. Model how to follow the rule and ask individual students to demonstrate. Use pictures or drawings to illustrate the rules.

A Classroom Signal
Establish a special signal with your students. This signal will be used throughout the year to mean "Stop. Look at me. Listen." The signal might be three handclaps, the ring of a small hand bell, a tap on the chalkboard, etc. Help the students understand that when they hear the signal they must *stop* what they are doing, *look* at you, and *listen.* (Some teachers have students put their hands on their heads when they hear the signal. This is a good way to assure that they stop what they're doing.)

Remember to use this signal many times during the first few days of school so that students will get used to obeying it. Later, use the signal whenever you want your students' attention. Be sure to explain why you asked them to stop, look, and listen!

It was getting too noisy. Please remember to speak in soft voices.

It's time to go to music class. Put your books away and get in line. Remember to walk, please.

It's time to listen to a story!

Classroom Helpers
Most students really enjoy helping the teacher. A student who feels that he or she never gets a turn to help will feel hurt or left out. A Helper Chart will ensure that everyone gets a chance.

Before you make your Helper Chart, decide what helpers you want. Do you want students to pass out papers? Do you need line leaders to avoid the problem of who will be first in line? Helpers can make sure books are back on the shelves, toys are in their boxes, and puzzles are put away. Do you have a fish or other pet in the classroom? Who will feed it? Who will check to see that there are no papers on the floor? That chairs are pushed under tables? Who will take the attendance slips to the office? Erase the chalkboard? All of these jobs can be assigned to daily or weekly Classroom Helpers and recorded on a Helper Chart.

Making a Helper Chart
A chart such as the one shown can be made on a bulletin board or on a large piece of corkboard or tagboard. Make drawings or cut out pictures to help illustrate the jobs on your Helper Chart. Put a card with each student's name in a box or envelope so you will always have them handy. Go over the chart with the class to make sure everyone understands the duties of each Classroom Helper.

Using the Helper Chart
On Monday, put a card with a student's name next to each job. If necessary, review what each helper is to do. If you expect each helper to do his or her job well, it will happen! Be sure to offer praise and encouragement.

On Friday, as you take the names down, write on the back of each card the job that student had. After everyone has had a turn at being a helper, you can start again. Look at the back of the cards to make sure you give the children different jobs than they had before.

Helper Hats or Badges
If you're working with small children, they will enjoy wearing Helper Hats or Helper Badges. A Helper Hat can be easily made by cutting a strip of paper long enough to fit around a child's head. Paste a symbol of the helper on the strip—a stamped envelope for the "mail carrier" who takes the attendance slips to the office, a picture of a crayon for the helper who puts the crayons away, a large numeral 1 for the line leader, etc. (See page 18 for badge patterns.)

As an alternative, you might make Helper Badges. To make Helper Badges, draw or paste appropriate pictures on squares of cardboard or three-by-five cards. Punch a hole at the top of the card and string it on a piece of yarn long enough to go around a student's neck. (You might cover the cards with adhesive plastic to make them more durable.)

At the end of each day, collect the hats or badges and place them near the Helper Chart so they're ready for the following morning.

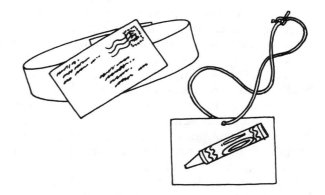

Establishing a Daily Routine
You will find it very helpful to establish a daily routine with which to begin your class. By doing certain things every day, you allow your students to become very familiar with the materials, concepts, and language. The children will feel secure and at ease in their new language because they know what to do and say. When students feel successful, they will be encouraged to communicate in English. This means that the probability of their wanting to participate in other activities in which they speak English will be very high.

As you develop your daily routine, you will want to choose a variety of activities which allow your students to participate in different ways—repeating, describing, answering questions, asking questions, explaining, etc. Once you have chosen four or five brief activities, decide in which order you will do them. If you do the same activities in the same order every day, you will establish a routine through which your students will know that class has started and it's time to settle down, have fun, and participate in English.

▶ When you have a daily routine to start the class, everyone knows what he or she must do, and there's less opportunity for confusion and wasted time. Children like knowing what the limits are, and even small children like knowing what comes next! A daily routine helps them develop a sense of time.

If you looked through this book and marked some activities as suggested in How to Use This Book, you might look back at them again. If you have not yet marked activities, you might do so now. Think about the activities you chose. Will they allow your students to participate in different ways?

It's important for EFL/ESL students to have many opportunities to speak. If you do activities that the children think are interesting and fun, they will naturally want to join in. Will the class starter activities you chose be fun for the students? Will the materials that you'll use be different for each activity?

For EFL/ESL students, feeling secure in a routine and knowing what they should do next reduces their anxiety and allows them to participate more fully. The activities that you choose for your daily routine should allow children to talk about certain things every day, so that talking about these things in English becomes as automatic as it is in their mother tongue. When the activities are fun, the children love to participate!

▶ It is our responsibility as EFL/ESL teachers to motivate our students to speak in English. When we use attractive materials and activities that are enjoyable but not too difficult, and when we ourselves are having fun, our students will participate easily!

After establishing a routine, we must be careful to anticipate when our students are no longer enjoying an activity. Often, just by changing how an activity is conducted, we can spark new interest.

(For example, choose a student to be the teacher. Being able to use the pointer has inspired many wiggly students to pay attention and participate!) Nothing is worse than having to take part in an activity that has become dull and boring. Don't let that happen! Be ready to change activities when you see that it's necessary.

After students become familiar with the daily routine, let them do the activities on their own. When students feel comfortable with an activity, it's exciting to see them "take off"!

In fact, as you continue with the daily routine, you will find that the activities can become less and less teacher directed. When your students begin to do activities on their own, you will know that they are acquiring the new language!

If your class must participate in assemblies, open classrooms, or end-of-the-year performances, allow them to do activities they are very familiar with. Parents and supervisors will be overjoyed as they see the students participating with ease and self assurance.

▶ It has been researched and proven that a person performs best when his or her anxiety level is low. When students feel comfortable with the materials and activities, their ability to communicate in their new language will be much higher than if they are put into an unfamiliar situation.

If your students are especially interested in a particular activity, encourage them to do the activity as a project at home and later to present it to the class. Many of the activities in Observing Our World are suitable for at-home projects.

You might find it useful to end your class with a daily routine also. This will help children know that class is over and will reinforce their confidence that they are really learning.

▶ Remember that as EFL/ESL teachers, we must make sure our students *want* to communicate in English. Take advantage of all opportunities to help children enjoy learning their new language.

Attendance

Most schools require teachers to keep a record of their students' attendance. As we all know, this can be a time when students get distracted, and we can waste a lot of time trying to regain their attention. But if you make these few minutes fun, the students won't mind listening as you call roll, and you'll be starting your class in a positive way.

Attendance Chart

Divide a bulletin board or a large piece of tagboard into three long sections. Put a picture of a boy at the top of one section, a picture of a girl at the top of another section, and a picture of a house at the top of the third section. (See pages 3 and 4 for patterns.)

Make a name card for each student and pin or tape the cards to the third section of the chart, under the house. (If you make your chart out of tagboard, you might cover it with plastic. This will enable you and the children to attach the name tags to the chart with masking tape.)

As you call roll, each child's name should be taken from below the house and placed under the boy or the girl. You might do this yourself, you might ask a specific child to do it each day, or each student might find and move his or her own name from "home" to "school."

As you call the roll, lead a conversation in English. This will get students used to hearing the language and remind them that this is the English class. Say, for example:

> Is Tony here today?
> *Yes, he is.*

Is Tony a boy or a girl?
> *He's a boy.*
Put Tony under the boy.

Is Maria here today?
> *No, she's not.*
Maybe Maria is sick.
We won't put Maria in school today.
Maria is staying at home.

After you finish taking roll, help students count how many boys came to school today, how many girls came to school, and how many children stayed home. Ask:

How many boys/girls are in school today?

How many boys/girls are at home?

How many children are in our class?

Are there more boys or girls in our class?

Did more boys or girls come to school today?

At the end of the day, put all the children's names back in the "home" section of the chart. You might say good-by to each child as you move his or her name from "school" to "home."

Name Games

Make a name tag for each child. (See page 4 for patterns.) The tags might be pasted onto thin cardboard for durability. For very young children, the tags can be fastened to clothing with masking tape.

Older children might tape or glue safety pins to the backs of the tags.

If your students are young, pass out the name tags each day. Show each tag, read the name, and hand it to the correct student. Soon children will begin to recognize their own names and those of their classmates.

For older students, you can have a silent roll call. As you hold up each name tag, the correct student must stand or raise his or her hand. Mix the cards up every day, so students must pay attention and watch for their names.

When the students can read the names easily, hold up two name tags at a time. The two students named must stand up and greet each other, using whatever greeting patterns you have presented.

Hello, Tony.
Good morning, Maria. How are you?

Roll Call Responses

Instead of always having children answer "Here" or "Present" when you call their names, think of interesting ways for them to respond. For example, they might clap, stand up, or raise both hands. They might name a favorite food, color, television program, song, actor, singer, etc. They might all stand and then sit down as their names are called. By asking for a variety of responses, you can turn a boring task into an enjoyable one.

You can practice specific sentence patterns by asking students to respond to their names in complete sentences. Some examples are:

I want to ———.

I like ———.

I don't have ———.

As the students acquire more English, you can increase the difficulty of the response to the roll call. For example, you might ask students to name:

1. Something nobody else has said that we will put (in our suitcase/in our supermarket cart/in our new house/on our farm).
2. Something that is (bigger/smaller) than the last item named (*ant, fly, grasshopper, mouse, hamster, kitten, dog,* etc.; *dinosaur, house, elephant, camel, car, lion,* etc.).
3. A word that describes (*soft, big, purple, ugly,* etc.).
4. The word that means the opposite of one that you say (*hot/cold, big/little, black/white, in/out,* etc.).

▶ The few minutes you spend taking roll can provide a useful review of the vocabulary you will work with in class that day.

Recording Attendance

Choose a different student each day to use your class list and record the attendance. This will encourage the others to cooperate as they will all want a turn.

If you must hand in a list of absent children to the office, allow a different child to do it each day.

▶ All children enjoy being helpers. By giving them instructions in English and asking them to describe in English what they are doing, you will be giving them practical, relevant practice in their new language. See page vi for additional information on Classroom Helpers.

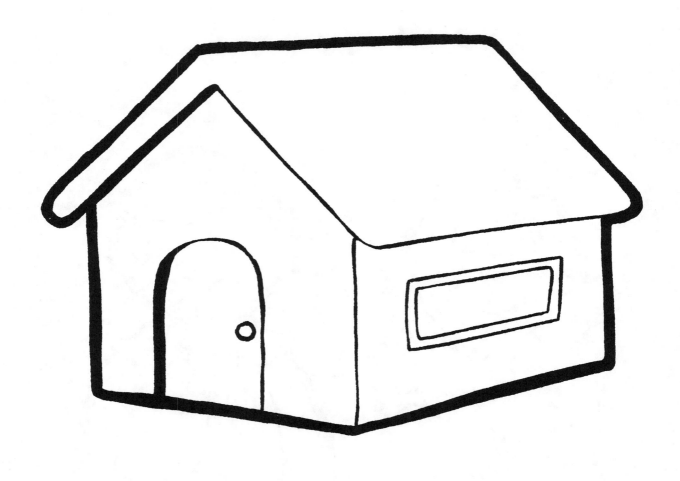

MY NAME IS

_____

MY NAME IS

_____

Calendar

JANUARY						
Sunday	Monday	Tuesday	Wednesday	Thursday	Friday	Saturday
1	2	3	4	5	6	7
8	9	10	11	12	13	14
15	16	17	18	19	20	21
22	23	24	25	26	27	28
29	30	31				

Use the calendar grid and the day, month, and number cards on pages 7, 8, and 9 to make a classroom calendar. You may duplicate the grid to make a new calendar for each month, or you might cover the grid with plastic and reuse it. Pin or staple the grid to the bulletin board. You might paste the day, month, and number cards onto thin cardboard to make them more durable.

You will probably find it convenient to label three envelopes for the days, months, and numbers, and to attach them to the bulletin board near the calendar. This way, you will always have them handy.

Naming

At the beginning of each day, you will want to review the name of the day. You may wish to use a different method to do this each month.

1. You can start each day by naming the day and putting the correct card on the calendar. Take the card off at the end of the day.
2. You might begin each week by putting *Monday* on the calendar, adding *Tuesday* the next day, and so on until all the days of the week are on the calendar. (Help students name the weekend days and add them either on Monday or on Friday.) Take the cards off at the end of the week.
3. You might begin each month by putting the correct day on the calendar, adding cards day by day until all the days are up. On subsequent weeks of the month,

ask students to point to and read the correct day name.

As you put up or refer to the name of each day, you might ask questions to practice verb tenses.

What day was it yesterday?

What day will be tomorrow?

What did we do on Monday?

What are we going to do on Friday?

After students name the day of the week, help them say the date and put the correct number on the calendar grid. Once students can recognize and name the numbers, they will enjoy finding the correct one and putting it up.

As students work with the numbers, ask such questions as:

What number is this?

What number comes after nine?

Does the nine go before or after the eight?

Days and Months

Attach strings to Days of the Week Cards (see page 10) so children can wear them around their necks. Give seven children the day tags and have them stand at the front of the room. The rest of the class should give directions to put them in the correct order.

Tom has Sunday. Tom is first.

Maria has Monday. Maria goes next to Tom.

5

After the students are in correct order, ask the class to name the days in sequence. Each child at the front must raise both hands when his or her day is named. Make similar cards for the months and repeat the activity.

Pin or tape a day or month card to a student's back. That student must ask questions to determine what day or month it is. For example:

Am I a day?

Am I before Tuesday?

Am I after Sunday?

You might also have other students give clues, such as:

You go to music class on this day.

We don't go to school in this month.

As students become confident of the days of the week and the months of the year, challenge them to name the one you skip as you recite the days or months in order. Later, individuals will enjoy being the leader for this game.

As students' English improves, ask riddles about the days and months. For example:

What (day/months) begin with *m*?

Which is the (first/last) month of the year?

What (day/month) comes (before/after) (Tuesday/June)?

Teach students these popular calendar rhymes.

Thirty days have September,
April, June, and November.
All the rest have thirty-one,
Except for February, which has twenty-eight
And in leap year twenty-nine.

How many days has my baby to play?
Friday, Saturday, Sunday,
Monday, Tuesday, Wednesday, Thursday,
Friday, Saturday, Sunday.

Weather

Duplicate the weather cards on pages 11 and 12. Pin them on the bulletin board or tape them on the chalkboard. Each day, ask what the weather is like. Then let a student put a colored pin or a check mark after the appropriate weather card. At the end of the month, help the children count how many sunny days, how many windy days, etc., there were that month. Students might make a weather chart to keep track of the weather each month. Which month had the most sunny days, the most rainy days, etc.? (There are many additional suggestions in the Weather section of this book beginning on page 30.)

Birthdays and Special Events

You might help students make a chart to show when each child's birthday is. Which month has the most class birthdays? Start the day by singing "Happy Birthday" to the birthday child. (There are many additional suggestions in the Happy Birthday! section of this book beginning on page 28.)

On days that you have "special events," such as a class outing, assembly, visitor, etc., note it on the classroom calendar. At the end of the week, the students might write about the event or draw a picture of it. At the end of the month, display the stories or drawings and help students recall the special things that happened that month.

Bulletin Board Ideas

Each month, label the bulletin board near the calendar with the topic students will be learning about—zoo animals, community helpers, vehicles, etc. Students can cut out or draw appropriate pictures to display. Use the bulletin board for a quick vocabulary review at the start of each day's class.

For a unit on shapes, put large shapes cut out of paper on the bulletin board. (See page 19 for patterns.) At the beginning of each class, ask two or three children to name a shape. When a child names a shape correctly, he or she may sign that shape. (There are many additional suggestions in the Shapes section of this book beginning on page 23.)

For a unit on food, help the students make a graph to show what each person ate for breakfast or brought for lunch. Fill in the chart at the beginning of class. Which foods are the most popular with the children in your class?

JANUARY	FEBRUARY	MARCH	APRIL	MAY	JUNE	JULY	AUGUST	SEPTEMBER	OCTOBER	NOVEMBER	DECEMBER

Sunday	Monday	Tuesday	Wednesday	Thursday	Friday	Saturday
1	2	3	4	5	6	7
8	9	10	11	12	13	14
15	16	17	18	19	20	21
22	23	24	25	26	27	28
29	30	31				

SUNDAY

MONDAY

TUESDAY

WEDNESDAY

THURSDAY

FRIDAY

SATRUDAY

windy

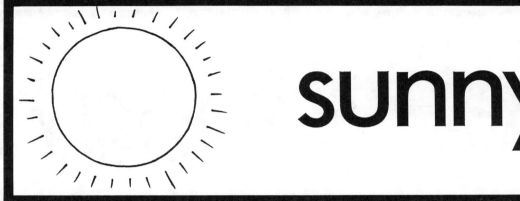

sunny

cloudy

rainy

From *EFL/ESL Class Starters,* © 1988, Scott, Foresman and Company.

11

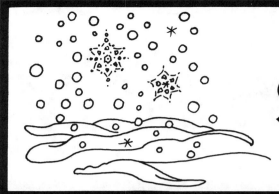 snowy

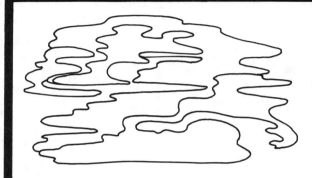 foggy

 Birthdays

 Special Days

Color of the Week

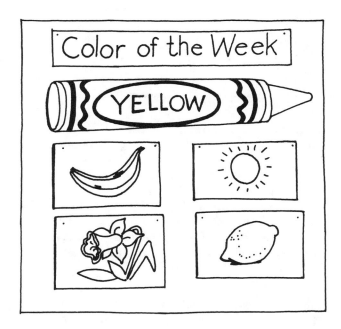

The more ways you can present concepts and vocabulary to your students, the more they will understand and practice the new language they are learning. Spend some time at the beginning of each day reviewing topics that you have already presented. This will help the students feel sure of themselves and of what they are learning, and it will remind them to use the language they know when presented with new topics.

Once you have presented words for colors, shapes, and sizes, your students will be able to use those words to describe anything. Help them master these concepts by working on them week by week. (If your students are very young—3 or 4 years old—you might want to spend more than a week on each topic.)

You will want to decide ahead of time what color you are going to present each week. Collect as many things as possible that are the chosen color—toys, pieces of cloth, clothing, magazine pictures, crayons, balloons, construction paper, buttons, foods, chalk, flags, etc. You will use all of them to present and reinforce the Color of the Week.

Make a Color Chart for the bulletin board. Make a large sign that says *Color of the Week*. Duplicate the crayon on page 17. Write the name of the color in the oval space and color the crayon the appropriate color. Put pictures of objects that are the chosen color under the crayon. Refer to the Color Chart throughout the week to reinforce the color of the week.

Monday

On Monday, show all the things you collected. Explain that you were looking for yellow things, and that these are the things you found. Hold up each item in turn and reinforce the name of the color.

> Look. I found this. It's yellow.
> This is yellow, too.
> Is this yellow or green?
> Is this yellow or black?
> What color is this?
> Who can tell me what color this is?
> Put your hand up if you know what color this is.

If possible, display all the yellow objects on a table. If you cannot do this, perhaps you can put them in a yellow box, bag, or basket so they will be handy all week.

At the end of class on Monday, tell your students to look at home and find something yellow. Ask them to bring it to school on Tuesday.

Tuesday

On Tuesday, ask each child to come to the front of the room and show what he or she brought. Prompt them to say whatever they can about the objects. Be sure to encourage and praise the children, even if they can do no more than name the color!

This is yellow.

I found something yellow.
I found this (ball).

I found this in my house.
It's yellow. Do you like it?

If any children forgot or were unable to find something, give them one of the yellow objects you collected. Don't let anyone feel left out!

Ask each child if he or she can leave the yellow object at school for the week. Put it with the rest of the yellow things. (You might want to tape the child's name to the object so it won't get lost.)

At the end of class on Tuesday, ask everyone to wear something yellow on Wednesday.

Wednesday

On Wednesday, ask each child to stand and to identify or point to his or her yellow clothes. (You will want to provide yellow paper hats for those students who don't wear something yellow. Or you might duplicate the crayon badge on page 18 and let students color it the appropriate color. The badges can be taped or pinned to the children's clothes.)

Children will enjoy following instructions if you present them as a game.

> If you're wearing a yellow sweater, stand up.
> If you're wearing yellow socks, clap your hands.
> If you're wearing a yellow hat, touch your nose.

You will want to adjust your directions according to the abilities of your class:

> Yellow sweaters, stand up!
> Everyone with yellow socks, clap your hands.
> Boys wearing yellow hats, touch your noses.

Help the class count how many students are wearing yellow sweaters, yellow socks, etc. You might make a chart or graph to show the results.

For additional counting and classifying activities, use the yellow objects you collected. First, ask a student, or a small group of students, to find all the yellow balls, flags, crayons, etc. When they have found them, ask them to show them to the class. Help students count the objects.

What do you have?
I have yellow flags.

How many yellow flags do you see?
I see five yellow flags.

At the end of class on Wednesday, tell students to look in magazines at home for pictures of things that are yellow. Ask each student to cut out three yellow pictures and paste them on a sheet of paper. (If students cannot find pictures, they might draw them.)

Thursday

On Thursday, ask students to show the pictures they found. You might do this in a question/answer format. (Students can respond by answering, by standing up, by holding up their pictures, etc.)

> Who found a yellow pineapple?
> Who found a yellow bus?
> Who found a yellow sun?

Ask the children to look around the room and find somebody else with the same yellow picture. Encourage them to name others with the same picture.

> I have a yellow banana.
> Tony has a yellow banana.

> I have a yellow flower.
> Maria and José have yellow flowers, too.

For more advanced classes, put the students in pairs. Each one should hold his or her picture so the other can't see it. Let the students ask each other questions to determine what the other has.

> I have a yellow bike. Do you have a yellow bike?
> *No, I don't.*

> I have a yellow flower. Do you have a yellow flower?
> *Yes, I do.*

> I have a yellow ball. Do you have a yellow ball?
> *Yes, I do.*

> You have a yellow flower and a yellow ball!

Friday

End the week with a treat on Friday. You might make lemonade and color it with the appropriate food color. (Students will especially enjoy blue or

there are colors of objects. Name the groups The Yellow Team, The Blue Team, etc. Ask each team to stand in a line. Explain that when you say a color, the first person on that team must go to the table and find something that color, run back, touch the next person on the team, and then sit down. Call out the names of the colors in random order. (To make it fair, you might put colored tokens or small pieces of paper in a hat and draw them out.) The first team with everyone sitting down wins.

For a different kind of team activity, divide the class into groups and assign each group a color. Everyone in the group might wear a badge or hat of that team's color. Give instructions such as the following:

Red, put your hands up.
Blue, clap your hands.
Green, stand up.
All colors, stand up.
Pink, run in place.
Blue, sit down.

To practice prepositions, gather objects of different colors. Divide the class into groups. Each group should have as many members as you have colors of objects. Give each member of each group a different-colored object. First, have students identify their colors.

Who has something yellow? Hold it up.

Show me something blue.

Now you are ready to give such instructions as:

Red, stand in front of blue.

Black, stand behind green.

Orange, stand between red and blue.

As the students move around to follow the instructions, ask such questions as, "Who is first in line? Who is next to green? Who is last?"

green lemonade!) At the end of the day on Thursday, help the children make a list of the things they will need to make the lemonade. If you want the students to bring ingredients, be sure to send notes home to the parents.

More Than One Color

After you have introduced several colors, you can add activities such as these.

Mix objects from several different weeks. Place the colored boxes, bags, or baskets they go in at the front of the room. Ask students to come forward and help you put the objects into the correct box. Perhaps each child could choose three objects and place them into the appropriate bag or box. Help them describe their actions according to their abilities.

(Child picks up object.) Yellow.
(Child puts object in box.) Yellow.

This is yellow. The box is yellow.

The yellow sweater is in the yellow box.

I have a yellow sweater. I'm putting it in the yellow box.

Mix objects from several weeks and place them on a table. Divide the class into as many groups as

Color Rhymes

Children will enjoy learning these nursery rhymes during the appropriate weeks. You might give students a brief explanation of the rhymes, but remember that when English-speaking children learn them, they do not understand all the words.

Mary had a little lamb;
Its fleece was white as snow;
And everywhere that Mary went,
The lamb was sure to go.

Mary had a pretty bird,
With feathers bright and yellow
And slender legs—upon my word,
He was a pretty fellow!

Higgledy, piggledy, my black hen;
She lays eggs for gentlemen.
Gentlemen come every day
To see what my black hen did lay.

Dickery, dickery, dare,
The pig flew up in the air.
The man in brown soon brought him down.
Dickery, dickery, dare.

Little Boy Blue, come blow your horn.
The sheep's in the meadow, the cow's in
   the corn.
Where is the boy who looks after the sheep?
He's under a haystack, fast asleep.

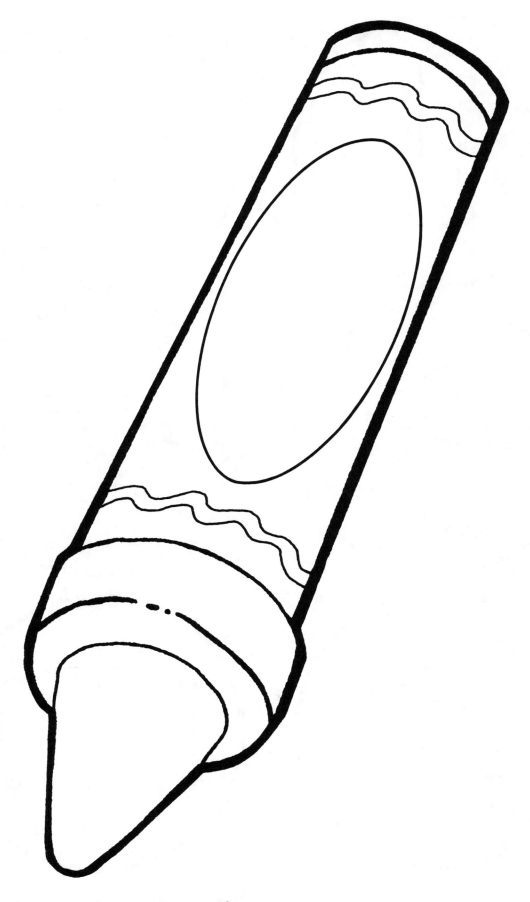

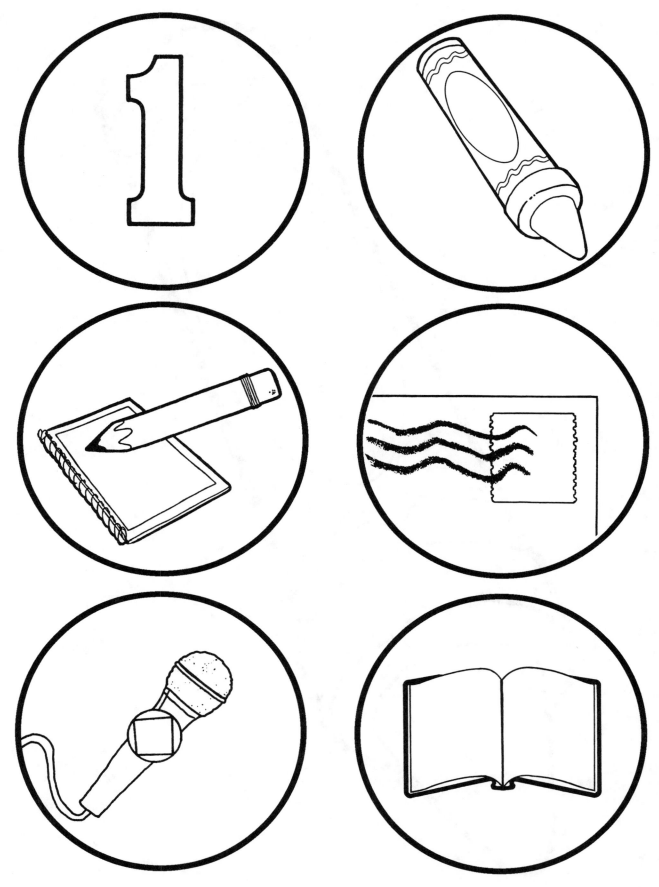

Color the △'s red.

Color the ○'s blue.

Color the ▢'s yellow.

Color the ▢'s green.

How many △'s? _____   How many ▢'s? _____

How many ○'s? _____   How many ▢'s? _____

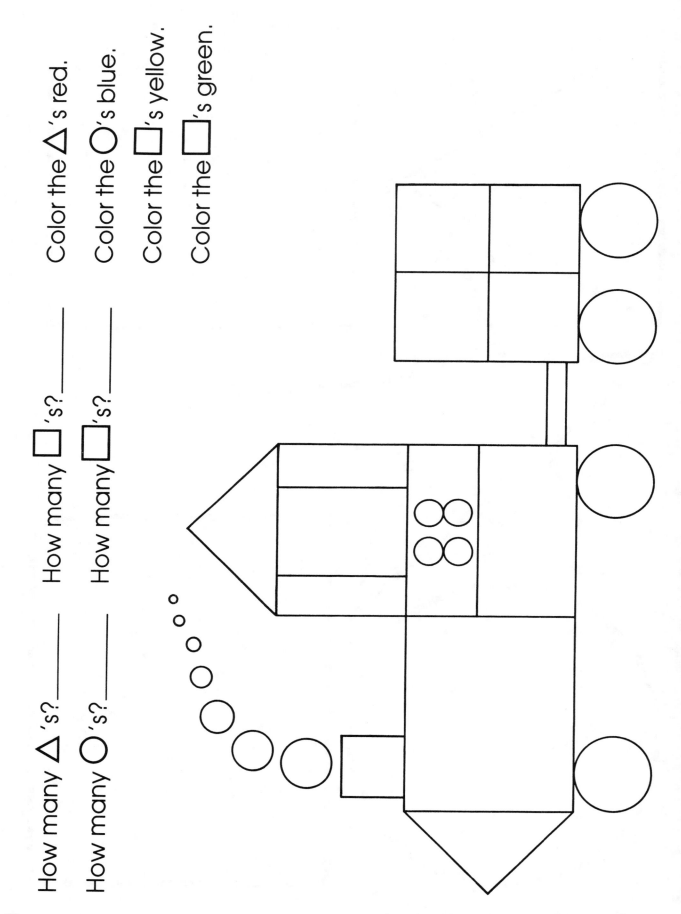

From *EFL/ESL Class Starters,* © 1988, Scott, Foresman and Company.

It's my birthday!

22

Shapes

Shape of the Week

You can use the week-by-week procedures described in Color of the Week to present any group of concepts and words. Here are suggestions for presenting shapes.

As with colors, decide ahead of time what shape you will work with that week. Draw the shape on the chalkboard. You will want to provide examples of the shape cut out of colored paper, along with wooden or plastic shapes if possible. (Use the patterns on page 19.)

Monday

On Monday, name the shape for the class. Point to the shape drawn on the board, show paper and plastic shapes, etc. Then ask students to look around the classroom to find things that have that shape. When they see something with the correct shape, they should stand and put their hands on their heads. After a few minutes, ask individuals to go and point to the things they saw (a clock, a doorknob, a phone dial, the wheel on a toy car, etc., for *circle*, for example). Help them identify what they found.

> I found a circle.
> Here's a circle.

When all the circles have been identified, point to the group near one object and ask the rest of the class:

What did they find?
They found a circle.

Throughout the day, help students identify objects that are circles. You might help students cut circles out of paper and tape or pin them to their clothes. This will help them remember that it's Circle Week.

At the end of class on Monday, ask everyone to bring something to class on Tuesday that is the shape of a circle.

Tuesday

On Tuesday, ask students to show their objects and say what they are. Remember that, even though students may not be able to name their object in English, they can say something about it —*It's a circle.* Help the students name the objects if desired. Provide a place in the room to display the pictures and objects.

> I have a button. It's a circle

> I have a picture of a pie. It looks like a circle.

Wednesday

Have a drawing activity on Wednesday. You might provide each child with a sheet of paper on which you have drawn a circle. Let the students use the circle as the start of a picture. Encourage students to be imaginative. How many different things do they draw? Display the circle pictures on the bulletin board.

Another possibility is to ask students to draw pictures using as many circles as possible. When the drawings are finished, ask them to trade with a partner. Ask each student to count how many circles there are in the picture he or she holds.

I see three circles.

It's a car. It has four circles.

He drew a boat. The boat has seven circles.

Rosa's picture has twenty circles. It's a boy with twenty balloons!

Thursday

On Thursday, give each child a sheet of white paper. Ask the students to draw three circles and cut them out. Be sure to talk to children as they work. Even if they don't understand every word, they will be unconsciously absorbing their new language.

Are you drawing a boy?

Are you drawing circles?

How many circles are you drawing?

What are you doing now?

Karen is almost finished. Are you finished?

When the circles are all cut out, students can use them to make designs or pictures.

Provide several large sheets of colored cardboard or tagboard, or cover large pieces of cardboard with colored paper. Divide the class into groups and give each group one of the large colored sheets and some paste or glue. Explain that the children should paste the white circles onto the colored sheets to make pictures or designs. (You might ask students to sketch a picture or design before they begin.) Encourage the students to describe what they are doing as they work.

I want to put a circle here.

I'm putting my circle next to that circle.

Let's put two big circles there.

When the groups are finished, display the designs or pictures for the class. If a group makes a picture, help the class identify it.

Friday

As with colors, you might end Shape Week with a treat on Friday. Round cookies, slices of pineap-

ple, or round crackers with cheese could be a treat for Circle Week. You can make cinnamon sandwiches in the shapes of squares, rectangles, or triangles for other weeks. This is especially fun if you let the children make the sandwiches. Again, encourage them to describe what they are doing.

I'm cutting the bread. I'm making a triangle.

I'm putting butter on the bread.

I'm putting on the sugar and cinnamon.

I'm eating a triangle! It's good!

More Than One Shape

After you have presented several shapes, you will want to do activities to compare and contrast. Duplicate the Count and Color Activity on page 20 for each student. Help the students read the directions and complete the activity.

Provide different-colored shapes, or have students draw, color, and cut out paper shapes. To start the activity, students should have their shapes on their desks. Then they must listen and follow your instructions.

Show me a circle.

Show me a green shape.

Who has a blue shape? What is it?

Put a red shape on your nose. If it's a triangle, say 'Hooray!'

Each student should hold a colored shape (a red circle, a blue triangle, a green rectangle, etc.). Ask them to stand in a circle. Explain that when you call a shape, everyone holding that shape should step into the middle of the circle. When you call the next shape, the ones holding that shape should step in; the ones already in the circle but not holding that shape must step back. Start the activity slowly, then move more quickly.

Blue triangles.

Yellow circles.

All red shapes.

Yellow squares and triangles.

As students' knowledge of English increases, you can make the game more complicated by adding sizes.

Big squares.

Red squares.

Big green triangles.

All little shapes.

To prepare for the next activity, tape different-colored and different-sized shapes all over the classroom. Put the students into pairs. One student must describe a shape for the other to find. Let the partners take turns giving and following directions.

Find a blue circle.
  Here's a blue circle. It's on the window.
  Now you find a little rectangle.
I see a little rectangle. It's on that chair.

Show and Tell

Children enjoy talking about the things that are important to them. Favorite topics are new brothers and sisters, pets, birthdays, visits to the doctor, lost teeth, TV programs, new toys, trips, etc. By allowing two or three children to tell about something important to them at the beginning of each day, you will make your classroom an interesting place to be.

However, talking in front of the group in English is not easy! The children need lots of help.

Holding an object or picture for the class to see is one way to make talking in front of the class easier. A shy student can focus attention on the object and not on him- or herself. Pre-school children will feel more comfortable if they can sit on your lap as they speak.

At the beginning of the year, it is important to let students speak on a volunteer basis. If they are reluctant to try, you might begin each day by showing an object yourself and telling about it.

This is my new ruler.

It's long. It's blue.

I like my new ruler.

After you have given a few examples of what students can say, they will be ready to participate.

Students love working with puppets. Another way to help them overcome their shyness is by letting them speak through a Show and Tell Puppet which can easily be made using a sock or two pieces of cloth sewn together.

At first, you will want to help students talk about their objects or drawings by asking them questions that you know they can answer.

What do you have?

What color is it?

Did you get it for your birthday?

Allow one-word answers, nods, or whatever indicates that the children understand. Remember that language skills improve with practice, and understanding questions is a very important part of learning a language.

Encourage other children in the class to participate by asking questions about the object, too. Always remember to thank the child who shared.

Once students lose their fear of speaking in front of the group (which they will do quickly with your help), they will enjoy showing their favorite toys, drawings of a new puppy, etc. You may even have to assign two or three children per day so that everyone gets a turn!

You might provide a box or basket of objects for students to use when they don't have things to bring from home. Talking about familiar objects gives students confidence and, as the year progresses, both you and they will be delighted by the additional things they can say about the objects.

▶ Always remember to help all of the students who come up for Show and Tell feel comfortable. It's not easy to speak in front of a group. It's especially difficult in a new language!

Surprise Box

A Surprise Box is fun for children of all ages! Use a large cardboard box with a top on it. Paint the box a bright color, and cut a hole in one end. The hole must be large enough for a student's hand to go in, but not so large that he or she can see the object. (If you prefer, use a bag or a large sock.)

Put an object inside the box and fasten the cover. Let individual students reach inside the box, feel the object, and try to guess what it is. Put a different object in the box each day. If the objects are interesting things that the children can name, they will be eager to have a turn to reach in the box.

A Surprise Box can provide a lot of fun while reviewing vocabulary. If your students are learning the names for shapes, put a plastic circle or triangle in the box. If you're working with classroom objects, put in a crayon, a pencil, or a piece of chalk. When you're talking about food, use a carrot, a banana, an apple, or an orange.

As students learn more English, ask them to describe the object before naming it; for example:

It's long. It's hard. It's a pencil.

It's little. It's square. It's an eraser.

Students might also describe the object and ask the rest of the class to guess what it is:

It's long. It's hard. We use it in school. We write with it. What is it?

They're little. They're round. We eat them. What are they?

An alternative would be for the class to ask questions of the student at the front to try to guess the object.

As students become more proficient at identifying items, place more than one in the box. Prompt children to tell how the objects are different.

This one is round. It's hard.
This one is hard, too. It's not round. It's flat.

Put four objects in the box. Help students fold sheets of paper in half and then in half again to make four squares. Let each one feel the objects in the box and then draw pictures of them. Which students can draw all four items correctly?

At the end of a week, you might ask students to draw pictures from your descriptions of things that have been in the Surprise Box that week. Have them fold paper as described above. Then give instructions for drawing:

Listen. This was in the box. It's an animal. It lives on a farm. It likes to play in the mud. It has a curly tail. It says 'Oink.' Draw a picture.

Students will continue to be interested in the Surprise Box if you continue to put interesting things inside. A few things you might start collecting are small plastic animals and vehicles; a spoon and a fork; a toothbrush and a comb; a belt; a baby shoe; pieces of cotton, wood, and sandpaper; paper clips, rubber bands, and erasers; cardboard or plastic letters and numerals; leaves, stones, and feathers, etc. Put in an ice cube in a sealed plastic bag. Put in a live guinea pig or kitten! You might also encourage students to bring items from home for the others to guess.

Happy Birthday!

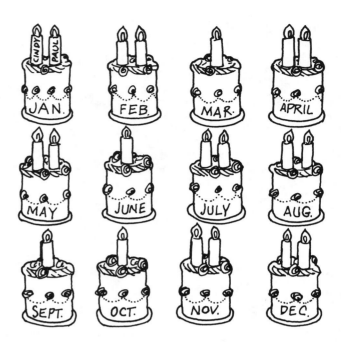

Birthdays are very special days! We can make each student feel special, and have lots to talk about, if we set aside time to celebrate birthdays. A birthday celebration is a great warm-up at the beginning of a day's work.

First, you will want to make a chart on which to record children's birthdays. You might do this at the beginning of each month in conjunction with making that month's calendar. (See the Calendar activities, page 5). Or you might start the year by making a chart that includes everybody's birthday.

Duplicate twelve copies of the birthday cake on page 21 and label one for each month. Write the names of the children who have birthdays during each month on the appropriate cake. Or duplicate a candle from page 21 for each child and put it on the appropriate cake. Display the cakes on the bulletin board.

Make a birthday crown for the birthday boy or girl to wear. If a crown is not appropriate for your students' age group, make a birthday badge. (See page 22 for patterns. Use the directions for Helper Badges and Helper Hats on page vii.) You might also make a ribbon banner for the birthday child to wear.

For children who have birthdays when school is not in session, you might celebrate six months from their real birthdays. If you have many children in your class, you might have one Happy Birthday Day each month to celebrate all that month's birthdays.

Birthday Cakes

Many schools allow you to celebrate birthdays by having children bring in cake or cookies. Children love this kind of treat and will enjoy talking about it. If this is not possible, or as a supplement to this, children can make pretend cakes.

Duplicate the cake and candles on page 21. Label the cake with the birthday child's name and help him or her color it and tape the correct number of candles on it. Display the cake on the bulletin board. Or you might duplicate a copy of the cake for each student. Let the children decorate the cakes with crayons, stickers, etc., and present them to the birthday child to take home.

You can also make a "cake" out of a cardboard box with a lid on it. Let the students color the box or decorate it with pictures, pasted-on candies, etc. Cut holes or slits in the top so you can put candles (real or cardboard) on the cake. Again, help the birthday child add the correct number of candles. Make sure to let him or her make a wish and "blow out" the candles.

Birthday Cards

Children enjoy making birthday cards for one another. They might do this in class or at home. As students complete their cards, they can put them inside the birthday cake box described above. Present the cake to the birthday child to take out the cards and read them.

You might also show students how to fold a sheet of paper in half and draw a "birthday present" inside. Help them think of things the birthday child will really like. When they are finished, let the class sit in a circle with the birthday child in the middle. Each student can hand his or her "present" to the birthday child and say, "Happy birthday." The birthday child should open the present, name it, and say whatever he or she can about it. Help the children remember to say, "Thank you."

> It's a red bike! Red is my favorite color!
> Thank you, Alex.

Birthday Posters

Ask each child to make a poster showing things he or she likes. They can draw pictures, cut them out of magazines, or bring photographs from home. Display each child's poster on his or her birthday. The child can use the poster to tell the class about what he or she likes and wants for his or her birthday.

> Here's my bike. I like my bike.
> This is my doll. It was a present last year.

One or two children can use the poster to describe the birthday child, or the class can ask the birthday child questions about the things pictured. Even very shy children will enjoy using their posters to talk about themselves.

Birthday Games

Wrap familiar objects or put them in bags, or clip sheets of paper over familiar flashcards. Have the children sit in a circle. Play some music and have the children pass a "present" around the circle. When the music stops, the child holding the present must open it and identify it. Continue with other objects.

You might also wrap a small object with several layers of paper. Have the students pass the object around as described above. When the music stops, the child holding the "present" gets to take off one layer of paper. The game continues until the object is finally unwrapped and identified.

Students will enjoy celebrating birthdays by playing any favorite games—Bingo, Musical Chairs, guessing how many candies are in a jar, etc. Be sure to encourage conversation in English as you play. And be sure to sing "Happy Birthday to You."

Planning a Party

Whatever you do to celebrate birthdays, you will want to involve your students in the planning. You can provide many opportunities for conversation by talking about what you will eat and drink, what games you will play, etc. Let groups of children work together to make lists of what you will need. Put individuals in charge of food, games, and clean up. Everyone likes to be responsible for something!

Weather

IN NOVEMBER, HOW MANY DAYS WERE _____?

☼ sunny	𝄄 𝄄 𝄄
windy	𝄄
cloudy	𝄄
rainy	𝄄 𝄄
snowy	
foggy	
Birthdays	𝄄 𝄄 𝄄
Special Days	𝄄 𝄄

pins

The weather affects everyone. Talking about the weather provides a wealth of opportunities for language practice. In addition to "weather words" such as *sun, cloudy,* and *raining,* students can use descriptive adjectives (*cold, hot, nice, terrible*), talk about clothing (*raincoat, sunglasses, boots*), and activities (*flying kites, making snowmen, going to the beach*), or practice past, present, and future tenses (*last week, today, tomorrow*).

Talking about the weather at the beginning of class each day will help you focus your students' attention. You may wish to include a daily weather report in your classroom newspaper (page 46).

You will want to provide many pictures showing different kinds of weather, clothes, and activities. Do not try to teach all the weather vocabulary at once. Present a few words at a time and help students understand them before adding more. Show a particular picture more than once, each time adding to the language the children already know.

Weather Wheel

You might begin the day's discussion of the weather by using the weather wheel on page 33. Pin the wheel to the bulletin board so it can spin around. (You may wish to paste the wheel onto thin cardboard for durability.) Pin or staple the arrow marked *today* so it points at the weather wheel. Ask what the weather is like today. (You might let one or more children go look out a window to determine the weather right now.) You can cue answers by asking questions:

Is it sunny?

Is it raining?

Is it cold out?

Prompt students to answer in complete sentences:

It's sunny today

It's not cold out.

The wind is blowing.

Then help students decide which picture on the weather wheel should be turned toward the arrow.

To practice verb tenses, you might make extra copies of the weather wheel for *yesterday* and *tomorrow.* Pin them on the bulletin board with the *yesterday* and *tomorrow* arrows. As students discuss the weather each day, ask them to remember what the weather was like yesterday and turn the wheel accordingly. What do they think the weather will be like tomorrow? Predicting the weather can be lots of fun!

Weather Charts

Let the children work in groups to make charts for different kinds of weather. Assign each group a certain kind of weather, or let the group choose the weather it wants to show. The children can draw pictures, use copies of the weather and season cards on pages 11, 12, and 36, and/or cut pictures out of magazines to put on their charts. Encourage them to find or draw as many different activities, clothes, etc., as possible that go with the weather they are showing. Help them describe the pictures as they paste them on the chart.

> It's hot. The children are swimming.

> She's wearing a raincoat. It's raining.

Weather Monkey

Cut out the weather monkey and the clothes on pages 34 and 35. Color them and cover both sides with adhesive plastic so you can dress and undress the monkey. You might also cover a piece of tagboard with adhesive plastic so the monkey and the clothes can be kept on display. Remember to make the clothes colorful so you can practice and review the color words.

At first, you will want to model appropriate language for the class.

> It's hot out. The monkey wants to wear shorts. I'm putting the shorts on the monkey.

Later, you can ask questions for the students to answer as they dress the monkey.

> What's the weather like?

> What does the monkey want to wear?

> Does the monkey want to wear long pants?

Finally, you can expect the children to make up sentences about the monkey on their own.

Younger children especially love this activity! They are eager to get a turn to dress the monkey according to the weather.

If the weather where you live doesn't change much according to the season, you may want to make several sets of clothing so the children can change the color of the monkey's sweater, shorts, etc. Or you might make a duplicate monkey. Tell the students it's the monkey's cousin who lives in a place where it snows. Older students might enjoy making additional clothing out of colored paper, scraps of fabric, etc.

Encourage students to draw pictures of things the monkey might do in different kinds of weather. Children who have acquired enough English might invent adventures for the monkey. These can be illustrated as a picture sequence or written as stories. Display the pictures or stories for the class to enjoy.

▶ Encourage students to express themselves in English, even if they don't know all the words! Offer whatever help they need.

Weather Cards

Use the weather and season cards from pages 11, 12, 36, and 37 to talk about the weather. (If your students cannot read English, cut the words off the cards.) Let the students match a Season Card (spring) with a Weather Card (windy) and a Seasonal Activity Card (kite). Ask what clothes they would wear to fly a kite on a windy spring day. Encourage them to talk about the cards they matched.

> It's spring. It's a windy day.
> I'm going to fly my kite.

> It's winter. It's snowing.
> I'm wearing my hat and mittens.

Make copies of the Seasonal Activity Cards for each student on page 37. Let the children color the cards and use them in an "information gap activity." After the cards have been colored, pair the students. Each one must try to find out what color the other's kite, umbrella, etc., is.

Duplicate copies of the Seasonal Activity Cards can be used to play Concentration. Place the cards face down on a desk or table. The first student turns over two cards and names them. If the cards are the same, the student gets to keep them. If they are different, he or she puts them back face down and the next child gets a turn. Who has the most cards at the end of the game?

Weather Graph

As you talk about each day's weather, the children can mark it on a graph. Tape or paste the weather cards down the left side of a large grid. Each day, let a student color the appropriate square for that day's weather. At the end of the month, students can count how many days were sunny, windy, etc. If you make a graph for each month, at the end of the year children can look back and see which month had the most sunny, rainy, windy, etc., days.

Even kindergarten children enjoy this activity, especially if you make it a privilege to color in the square for the day!

Weather Games and Activities

Help students cut out large tagboard clouds, raindrops, lightning bolts, snowflakes, and other weather symbols. Let them use these as props to act out the weather. For example, a student holding

the sun could walk behind a student holding a cloud and say:

I'm the sun. I'm hiding behind a cloud. It's a cloudy day.

Encourage the students to act out a summer storm, a windy spring day, a rainy spring day, etc.

Help the class make up and act out weather stories, using the tagboard symbols. Here is an example to get your class started.

One day it was very cloudy. The flowers were sad. They wanted to see the sun. Suddenly the sun peeked through the clouds. Soon the clouds went away. Then the flowers were happy. They liked the sun. The wind began to blow. The flowers danced in the wind.

Ask the children to pretend that their hands and fingers are raindrops. Let them tap their knees to show different kinds of rain—a soft drizzle, a warm summer shower, a bad thunderstorm. Encourage them to describe what each kind of rain feels like.

Let groups of children work together to think how they would act out things such as dawn or sunset, a rainbow, thunder and lightning, a snowstorm, etc. Let each group present its play or pantomime for the rest of the class.

If your students have never been in snow, it will be fun for them to learn about it. Help them find pictures, postcards, photographs, etc., of snowy scenes and of people doing "snow" activities—skiing, ice skating, etc. Show posters or movies of snowy places. Read books such as *The Snowy Day* by Ezra Jack Keats (The Viking Press, 1962).

▶ Remember that when you make difficult concepts come alive in your classroom, your students will remember them better. Bring in posters, movies, videos, books, etc., whatever you can. Children love them, so they are great teaching tools.

Children will always learn faster when they have real objects and experiences to talk about. Try to provide many kinds of clothing for different kinds of weather—raincoats, rainboots and snowboots, sweaters, jackets, winter coats and stocking caps, shorts, etc., for students to try on as they talk about the weather.

Let the children try on rainboots. Spray their feet with a hose.

Let the children put on mittens and give them ice cubes to hold. Ask them to pretend they are making snowmen. Encourage them to describe their actions and feelings.

Make ice-cream snowmen. Use chocolate chips for the eyes and mouths, colored candies for buttons, etc. Ask children to imagine playing in a big pile of ice cream. What would it feel like?

Ask the children to pretend they are snow skiing in the winter or water skiing in the summer. Help them describe how it feels.

If possible, provide a sand table so students can make sand castles. Encourage conversation as students put wet sand in a pail, turn the pail upside-down, etc. Provide containers in a variety of shapes for the children to use.

▶ Remember that these games and activities are not only fun in themselves. They also provide the opportunity to use weather vocabulary in new contexts. They give your students lots of chances to express themselves!

YESTERDAY

TODAY

TOMORROW

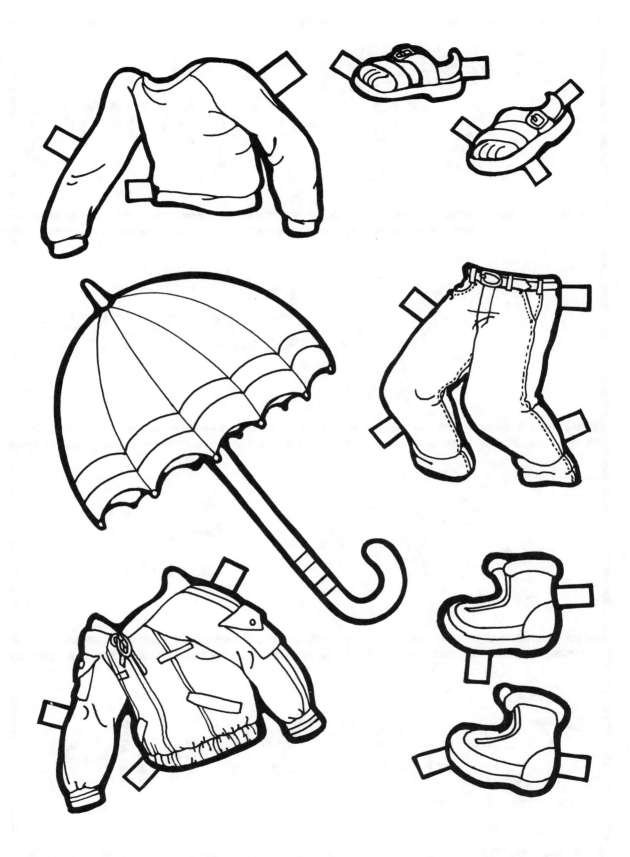

Spring

Summer

Fall

Winter

On the Way to School

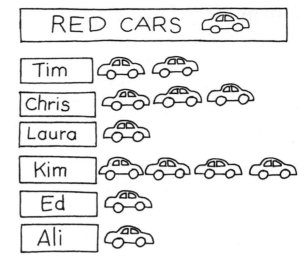

An assignment that is lots of fun for students to do and great for reviewing vocabulary is to ask them to look for things on the way to school. No matter whether the children walk to school or come in a car or bus, they can look for things, count things, and observe changes.

At the end of class every day, tell the students what to look for on the way to school tomorrow. Some ideas are:

Find something red/yellow/blue/etc.

Find something tall/short.

Find something that looks like a triangle/square/circle/etc.

Find something that is bigger than a car/bus/etc.

Find something that is smaller than a dog/refrigerator/etc.

Find something that is smaller than a car but bigger than a dog.

Find something that you can taste/smell/hear.

Find something that can jump/run/swim/etc.

Find somebody who's wearing a hat/running/etc.

Count how many dogs/cats/etc. you see.

Count how many blue/red/green cars you see.

Count how many tall buildings you see.

Count how many fountains/mountains/trees/police officers/bicycles/birds/animals/school buses/taxis you see.

See Year-Long Observations in the Observing Our World section of this book (page 40) for additional ideas.

Start each class by asking the children about the things they were supposed to look for. Some students may have forgotten, but as you continue doing the activity, more and more will remember. Be sure to praise those who do.

Who saw something red?
I saw a red car.
Did anybody else see a red car?
Stand up if you saw a red car.
Who saw something else red?
I saw a red umbrella.
I saw a red bike.

Another way to begin the class would be to ask the children to draw pictures of what they saw. Collect the pictures. As you show each picture, begin a conversation:

Who saw this?
I did. I saw three cats.

If you asked your students to count things, you might chart or graph the results. How many saw the same number of things? Who saw the most?

To practice *more than* and *fewer than*, write a number on the board; *five*, for example. Ask the children to say whether they saw more than five or fewer than five things.

After students become accustomed to looking for things on the way to school, ask them to suggest ideas. Individuals will enjoy having the whole class look for something they named!

Observing Our World

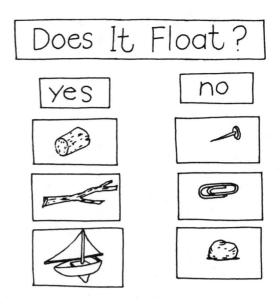

Observing is something that most children are very good at. They like watching things happen, and they like talking about them. Set aside a few minutes at the start of every day for an observation activity. Choose things that students will find interesting, and encourage them to talk! After each observation, let students record what happened by drawing pictures, making charts, or writing reports.

It's best to start with things that show change quickly. Young children enjoy holding a small piece of ice in their hands, feeling it, and watching it melt. Help them talk about the fact that the ice is hard and cold at first, then it turns to water. They can also observe that their hands were warm and dry, then cold and wet.

Does it Float?

Another quickly-done observation is an experiment to find out which objects float and which do not. If possible, use a clear glass container of water so everyone can see what happens. Let students take turns puttings things in the water to see if they float. Provide such items as a small sponge, a cork, a piece of paper, a toy boat, a leaf, a small piece of wood, a rock, a nail, a paper clip, etc. Encourage students to bring objects from home, too. Help them make a chart or bulletin board display to show which things float and which do not.

Encourage speculation about objects by handing someone an item and asking if he or she thinks it will float. Let the student test his or her theory.

Plants and Animals

Children like to grow and care for plants. They will be interested to find out that everyday seeds and beans will grow.

Line a glass with wet paper toweling. Place a few beans between the glass and the toweling. Remember to pour a small amount of water on the paper toweling every day to keep it moist. Within a few days the beans will begin to sprout. Help students observe the roots and the stem. How long does it take for leaves to form?

Orange or lemon seeds grow easily in a pot of dirt. Help students record how tall the plant is at the end of each week or month.

If possible, have students place a bird feeder outside the classroom. Encourage them to keep track of what kinds of birds come to the feeder, how

many birds come to the feeder each day, what each bird eats, etc. Do different kinds of birds come in the summer than come in the winter?

No matter where your students live, in the city or in the country, there will be some kind of animals to observe—wild animals, farm animals, zoo animals, or pets.

If you cannot keep an ordinary pet in your classroom, perhaps you could have an ant farm. Or you and the students might collect caterpillars. Cover the top or one end of a box with clear plastic and put the caterpillars inside. Be sure to include leaves from the plant on which you found the caterpillars. And be sure to punch air holes in the box! Students will be fascinated to watch the caterpillars make cocoons. And they will be delighted when the moths or butterflies emerge!

Anything Goes

By talking with your students and finding out what kinds of things they are interested in, you will think of many ideas for observing things and talking about them. Be creative, but remember that things that seem very ordinary can be fun to watch and discuss. A few more suggestions are:

1. Tape a leaf to a sheet of colored paper and put it in the sun for a week.
2. Put one plant on a sunny windowsill and another in a dark box for a week.
3. Put a shallow dish of water on a sunny windowsill and another in a freezer.
4. Put a stalk of celery in a glass of water and add food coloring.
5. Let students mail themselves stamped, self-addressed letters.
6. Put a piece of bread on a saucer and watch what happens for a week or two.
7. Use food coloring or water colors to mix new colors—what happens when you mix red and yellow? Red and blue?
8. Help children take pictures with an instant camera. experiment taking pictures with the lights on and off, indoors and outdoors.
9. Blindfold the children and give them small pieces of apple, pear, and potato to taste—can they tell the foods apart?
10. Watch the moon for a month.
11. Bring in a stopwatch. Find out who can hop across the room the fastest. How long does it take for everyone to find his or her red crayon?

Year-Long Observations

A year-long observation is not only interesting, it also provides many opportunities to add to students' vocabularies, to use a variety of verb tenses, etc. Different students in the class might be in charge of observing different things—the trees, plants, or birds near your school; the clothes people wear; the fruits being sold in the market; the sports children are playing; major news stories, etc.

Plan to discuss the observations on a specific day each month. A week before this day, remind the children to investigate and to record their findings. Young children can draw pictures and older ones can write brief reports. On "Observation Day," let the students share their findings with the class.

You will want to keep students' reports from month to month so they can compare similarities and differences. You might make an "Observation Calendar" on which you record significant information each month to help children remember what happened. Charts and graphs will also help students make comparisons.

Periodically, the students should summarize the information they have gathered.

The trees didn't change in January or February. In March they got leaves.

We saw butterflies in July and August. We didn't see any in November or December.

In October we had six rainy days. In November we had nine rainy days.

Fun With Numbers

When acquiring a second language, it is quite easy to learn to say the numbers in order. But it's very difficult to learn to manipulate numbers in any but one's native language! A few minutes of "number fun" at the beginning of class will enable students to learn not only to name the numbers in English, but also to work with them.

Make a large flashcard for each of the numerals. If possible, provide plastic numerals or numerals cut out of cardboard. And be sure to provide many things to count!

Identifying Numbers

You will want to present the numbers in order, a few at a time. For very young children, you may wish to teach the names of only three numbers at first. For older children, you might begin with five or ten.

After students can say the names of the numbers, show one flashcard at a time and say:

What number is this?
Clap/Jump this many times.
Show me this many fingers.

Number Sequence

These activities can be done with any sequence of numbers, depending on your class. You might use 1–10, 11–20, 1–20, 20–30, etc. You will want to begin with a short sequence, then add more numbers as students become more proficient.

Place the flashcards along the chalkrail in se-quence. Ask students to close their eyes. Take one or two cards away. Ask students to look at the cards and name the missing numbers.

Show one flashcard and ask:

What number is this?
What number comes before eight?
What number comes after eight?

Give ten students the flashcards for a sequence of numbers. Have them stand across the front of the room in mixed-up order. The rest of the class must give instructions to put them in correct sequence.

Bob has eight. Mary has seven. Bob, stand after Mary.

Tim has nine. Tim, stand between Bob and Laura.

Call ten students to the front of the room and give each a number flashcard. Make sure they don't let the other students see their cards. They should take turns giving their classmates clues until the numbers are guessed.

It's before nineteen.
It's after twelve.
It's before seventeen and after fourteen.

-teen and *-ty*

Most students will find it difficult to distinguish between such number words as *thirteen* and *thirty*. You will want to give them a lot of practice hearing and saying these words.

First, hold up flashcards with the numerals 13, 30, 14, 40, 15, 50, etc. Say the numbers, slightly exaggerating the accent on the first syllable of words ending in -*ty* and the last syllable of words ending in -*teen*. Ask the students to repeat. Begin slowly, then go more quickly as you gradually de-emphasize the accent.

After you have done a lot of practice in hearing and saying these numbers, dictate them in random order for students to write. Write the correct numbers on the board and let students check their own papers. Later, you can have them trade papers and check each other's work.

Arithmetic

If your students already know how to add, write some simple addition problems on the board and tell them how to read them in English:

> 2 + 2 = 4
> Two plus two equals four. (*Or:* two and two are four.)

When students feel comfortable reading the equations, dictate some simple addition problems for them to write and answer. Or you might write some problems on the board for students to add in their heads. Who can say the correct answer in English first? (You might divide the class into teams and do this as a contest.)

Similar games can be done with subtraction, multiplication, and division, once students have learned to do these.

As your students' proficiency increases, you can use simple word problems, either oral or written:

> You have six fish and two swim away.
> How many are left?

> You have two candies and I give you two more.
> How many do you have?
> You eat one candy.
> Now how many do you have?

At first, you will want to use props to help students understand these problems. Later, students will be able to do them in their heads.

Make cards with simple addition or subtraction problems such as: 3 + 2 = . Call one student forward and tape a card on his or her back. Let the rest of the class see the card. The students in the class should take turns giving clues until the one at the front guesses the answer and/or the equation.

Guess the Number

Get a small, glass jar. Every day, fill the jar with small objects such as crayons, candies, beans, paper clips, erasers, buttons, etc. Challenge the students to guess how many objects are in the jar. Each child can write his or her guess on a piece of paper. Then take the objects out and help the class count them. Who estimated correctly? Keep a record of how many of each kind of thing fits in the jar.

As students learn larger numbers, you can do the activity with a larger jar or box. Make a chart to compare how many of each object fit in each size jar.

Counting Rhymes

Children enjoy saying and acting out counting rhymes. You might give brief explanations, but don't worry if students don't understand every word.

> One, two, three, four, five,
> I caught a fish alive.
> Six, seven, eight, nine, ten,
> I let it go again.
> Why did I let it go?
> Because it bit my finger so!

> One, two, buckle my shoe;
> Three, four, shut the door;
> Five, six, pick up sticks;
> Seven, eight, lay them straight;
> Nine, ten, a big fat hen;
> Eleven, twelve, dig and delve;
> Thirteen, fourteen, maids a-courting;
> Fifteen, sixteen, maids in the kitchen;
> Seventeen, eighteen, maids a-waiting;
> Nineteen, twenty, my plate's empty!

Can students figure out the answer to the following riddle? (The answer is one—the narrator, who met everyone else coming from St. Ives.)

> As I was going to St. Ives,
> I met a man with seven wives.
> Every wife had seven sacks,
> And every sack had seven cats.
> Every cat had seven kits.
> Kits, cats, sacks, wives,
> How many were going to St. Ives?

How Do You Feel?

Everyone enjoys talking about himself or herself. Spending a few minutes at the beginning of class to talk about how everyone feels will elicit a lot of language, and it will be a lot of fun! You will want to encourage as many students as possible to participate. If they can't express their feelings in English, let them show them without words.

I'm happy today.

I hurt my arm.

I'm smiling because I'm happy.

I'm happy because I did all my homework last night, and I went to the movies.

I'm sad because I lost my sweater.

I don't feel well today. My head hurts.

I'm so excited! My cat had five kittens last night! They're cute! I love them.

I'm tired. I watched TV until ten o'clock last night.

Encourage individuals to come forward and act out how they are feeling. Students will enjoy both performing the pantomimes and trying to guess how others feel.

You're not sad.
You're not sleepy.
You're mad!

To practice asking questions, let the student at the front pantomime. Others should ask questions until they guess his or her feelings.

Are you happy/sad/sick/bored?

Do you want to laugh/cry/sleep?

Do you feel like smiling/singing/shouting?

Cut out the faces on page 38. Hold them up or tape them on the chalkboard one by one. As you hold up each one, ask students to raise their hands or to make a similar face if they feel the same way. Count how many students feel happy, sad, mad, sick, sleepy. Make a chart or write the results on the chalkboard:

Seven boys and girls are happy.
Two boys are sad.
One girl is mad.

Puppets

Cut out the faces on page 38 and tape them to sticks to make puppets. Students can use these puppets to show how they feel or to talk about their feelings.

This puppet is happy. It's smiling.
Can you make a happy face? Are you smiling?

Is this puppet happy or mad?
How do you look when you're mad?

How do you feel? Which puppet do you want?

Students can make larger, similar puppets by drawing faces on paper plates and taping them to sticks. You might provide buttons, bottle caps, yarn, pipe cleaners, ribbon, etc., for children to use to make the faces.

Hold up a series of puppets in rapid succession. Ask the students to imitate each puppet's face.

Divide the class into two groups. Show one group a puppet. The group must imitate the puppet's face. The second group must guess the feeling.

They're crying. They're sad.

They're frowning. They're mad.

They're laughing and smiling. They're happy.

Use the puppets to help students stretch their imaginations. Hold up a face and give such instructions as:

You're a bird. You feel like this.
What do you do?

What do mothers/fathers/babies do when they feel like this?

What would kangaroos do if they felt like this?

How would dogs bark if they felt this way?

▶ Remember, these activities might be noisy! Don't forget to have a signal that means "Stop. Look. Listen." (See page vi.) Reminding students to follow the Classroom Rules can help avoid chaos!

Here are some additional activities to help students understand and show feelings.

1. Ask them to walk/sit/stand as if they were happy, excited, tired, or mad.

2. Ask them to draw things that make them happy, sad, excited, bored. Let them compare their drawings.

3. Make feelings posters. Students can cut pictures from magazines that show happy/sad/angry/etc. people. Label a large piece of tagboard or a section of the bulletin board with a feeling; *happy*, for example. Let the students put up all the "happy" pictures.

4. Cut out eyes, noses, eyebrows, mouths, etc., from magazine pictures. Let the students assemble the parts to make happy/sad/mad/etc. faces.

Daily News

You can combine activities from every section of this book by "publishing" a class newspaper. The newspaper can include daily reports on the weather, birthdays, show-and-tell, observations, etc.

Begin by helping the class think of a name for the paper (*Daily News, Fifth Grade News, News from Our Class*, etc.). Write the name on tagboard or colored paper and pin it on the bulletin board. Each day's drawings or stories can be pinned below it. (An alternative is to stack five sheets of paper and pin them up. Each day's story should be written on the top sheet. That sheet can be torn off at the end of the day.)

Your students will enjoy sharing the newspaper with their families. Some weeks, you might allow a different child to take that day's newspaper home each afternoon. Other weeks, you might save the sheets until Friday and then review the week's events. The sheets can then be distributed for students to take home.

Reporting the News

If your students are young, they can report their news stories orally. Then you or the class should choose one or two stories to record in the paper. Ask the appropriate children to dictate their stories for you to write. Encourage them to draw pictures to illustrate the stories.

To help students understand how to report a story, you put on the reporter's badge (pad and pencil) from page 18 and report on something you

know your students will be interested in. Then let each child wear a badge as he or she reports a story. Or you might consider using a puppet as a class reporter. (Be sure the puppet wears a reporter's badge!) The puppet can give the first report every day to get things started. Shy children will feel more comfortable giving their reports through the puppet.

> Today is my baby brother's birthday.
> He's one year old.
>
> It rained last night.
> I walked in the puddles.
> My feet got wet.
>
> Our class did an experiment yesterday.
> We mixed different-colored paints.
> We mixed red and yellow to make orange.
> We mixed blue and yellow to make green.

At first, it's usually best to ask for volunteers to give the reports. Many children will be shy about talking in front of the group. Don't force them. With time, everyone will want to be a reporter. In fact, you might soon have the problem that everyone wants to report every day! It's best to allow only two or three children to speak per day. You don't want anyone to get bored!

▶ Remember that this activity should be fun. If too many children give reports, the activity will drag on and on, and it will be difficult for students to sit still and listen.

Older children can take turns writing reports. You should plan beforehand who is going to report